C000091510

SANTORINI :A TRAVEL GUIDE

ZION HALLEL

1

TABLE OF CONTENTS

Introduction

Nestled in the heart of the Aegean Sea, lies an enchanting island known as Santorini. With its idyllic landscapes, captivating history, and vibrant culture, Santorini has earned its reputation as a coveted destination for travelers seeking an otherworldly experience. As the morning sun bathes the island in a golden glow, and the gentle sea breeze caresses your skin, you will find yourself drawn into the magical charm that this paradise exudes.

From the moment you step onto the island, the sheer beauty of Santorini leaves you breathless. The iconic crescent-shaped Caldera, formed by a massive volcanic eruption ages ago, stands proudly as a testimony to the island's geological history. Whitewashed buildings, perched precariously on cliff edges, overlook the azure waters, creating a postcard-perfect scene that is etched in memory forever.

Beyond its mesmerizing scenery, Santorini is steeped in rich history and mythology. Known as the home of the ancient civilization of Akrotiri, the island has witnessed the rise and fall of ancient empires. Unearth the mysteries of the past as you explore archaeological sites, visit fascinating museums, and walk through cobbled streets that whisper stories of the past.

Santorini's allure is not limited to its physical beauty alone. The island boasts a vibrant and welcoming culture that celebrates its unique traditions and customs. Experience the warmth of the locals as you engage in lively conversations, savor traditional delicacies, and partake in colorful festivities that bring the community together.

Adventurers and leisure seekers alike will find solace in the myriad of activities Santorini offers. Delve into the depths of the Aegean Sea through scuba diving expeditions, or embark on a sailing journey around the island to witness its stunning cliffs from a different perspective. For those seeking relaxation, bask in the warm rays of the Mediterranean sun on the pristine beaches, or rejuvenate your senses at one of the island's luxurious spas.

In the evening, as the sun dips below the horizon, Santorini's beauty takes on a whole new dimension. The sky transforms into a canvas of mesmerizing hues, casting a magical spell on all who witness it. Take a leisurely stroll through the charming villages and savor delectable Greek cuisine as the stars begin to twinkle above, creating an ambiance that is nothing short of enchanting.

Santorini, with its compelling blend of natural wonders, historical significance, and heartfelt hospitality, remains an unparalleled destination that captures the hearts of visitors from all corners of the world. So, pack your bags and set foot on this enchanting island, for a journey to Santorini promises an experience that is nothing short of heavenly.

Chapter 1.

1.1 About Santorini

Santorini, an enchanting island in the Aegean Sea, beckons travelers with its captivating beauty and rich history. Nestled within the Cyclades archipelago, Santorini is renowned for its postcard-perfect landscapes, awe-inspiring sunsets, and unique architectural wonders.

As you approach the island, you are greeted by its iconic crescent shape, a result of a massive volcanic eruption that occurred several millennia ago. The sheer cliffs and multi-colored cliffs rising majestically from the azure waters create an unparalleled sight. Whitewashed buildings with vibrant blue domes dot the cliffs, adding a picturesque charm to the island's scenery.

The island's bustling capital, Fira, exudes a vibrant atmosphere, bustling with a mix of locals and visitors. Meandering through its labyrinthine alleys, you discover quaint boutiques, inviting cafes, and traditional tavernas, where you can indulge in mouthwatering Greek delicacies. A stroll along the rim of the caldera grants breathtaking views, leaving you mesmerized by the expanse of the Aegean Sea stretching far into the horizon.

Delving into Santorini's history, you uncover its ancient past dating back to the Minoan civilization. The archaeological site of Akrotiri offers a glimpse into this mysterious era, with well-preserved ruins and artifacts revealing the island's once-prosperous past.

As the sun begins its descent, you head to the charming village of Oia, famed for hosting the world's most stunning sunsets. Crowds gather at the cliffside to witness nature's masterpiece unfold, as the sun bathes the sky in a kaleidoscope of hues, casting a golden glow over the whitewashed buildings and crystalline waters below.

For adventure seekers, Santorini's volcanic origins provide a unique opportunity to explore the nearby islets of Nea Kameni and Palea Kameni. Hiking up the active volcanic craters presents an otherworldly experience, offering panoramic views of the caldera and the surrounding islands.

The island's allure extends beyond its physical beauty. The warmth and hospitality of the locals leave an indelible mark on your heart. Engaging in conversations with the friendly Santorinians, you gain insight into their traditional way of life, influenced by age-old customs and celebrations.

Whether you seek relaxation on pristine beaches, cultural exploration of ancient sites, or an enchanting escape into the realm of romance and charm, Santorini embraces every traveler with open arms. As the sun sets on your Santorinian adventure, you depart with a sense of awe and gratitude, carrying memories that will forever echo the magic of this exceptional island in the heart of the Aegean.

1.2 History and Culture

Santorini, an enchanting Greek island nestled in the Aegean Sea, boasts a rich tapestry of history and culture that weaves through the ages. This captivating destination is renowned for its stunning sunsets, charming white-washed buildings, and breathtaking volcanic landscapes, but beneath its picturesque surface lies a story that spans thousands of years.

Ancient History:
The island's history dates back to ancient times, where it was known as Thera. The Minoan civilization flourished here around 2000 BCE, leaving behind remnants of their sophisticated

society. Excavations at the archaeological site of Akrotiri have unearthed well-preserved frescoes, pottery, and evidence of advanced urban planning, hinting at a thriving ancient city lost in the volcanic eruption that shaped the island's present-day caldera.

Greek Influence:
Santorini's history intertwined with Greek mythology as it is believed to be the remnants of the lost city of Atlantis, mentioned in Plato's dialogues. The island played a crucial role in the Aegean trade routes and was a part of several Greek city-states, including the ancient city of Thera. The influence of Greek culture is still evident in the island's architecture, cuisine, and festivities.

Mediaeval Era:
During the mediaeval era, Santorini fell under the rule of various empires, including the Byzantine Empire and the Venetian Republic. The island's fortified villages, known as "kastelia," were built to protect the inhabitants from pirates and invaders. These distinctive structures, with their labyrinthine alleys and blue-domed churches, stand as a testament to the island's tumultuous past.

Cultural Fusion:

Throughout its history, Santorini has experienced the influences of different civilizations, creating a unique cultural blend. This fusion is evident in the local cuisine, which features delicious Mediterranean dishes infused with flavors from the Middle East and Asia. Traditional celebrations like the "Panigiria" showcase Greek music, dance, and customs, adding to the island's vibrant cultural scene.

Modern-Day Santorini:
Today, Santorini is a world-famous destination, attracting travelers from across the globe. Its captivating beauty, combined with its historical significance and warm hospitality, makes it an unparalleled experience for visitors. Despite the influx of tourists, the island's inhabitants remain deeply connected to their heritage, preserving their customs and traditions for future generations.

In conclusion, Santorini's history and culture intertwine like the vibrant threads of a tapestry, creating a captivating destination that delights the senses and nourishes the soul. Exploring the ancient ruins, strolling through the quaint villages, and savoring the local delicacies all contribute to the profound allure of this enchanting island, where the echoes of the past resonate with the present.

1.3 Best Time to Visit

Santorini, the picturesque Greek island in the Aegean Sea, is a dream destination for many travelers seeking sun-kissed landscapes and captivating vistas. Choosing the best time to visit this enchanting island depends on your preferences and what kind of experience you desire.

Spring (April to May) is a delightful time to explore Santorini. The island's beauty blossoms with colorful wildflowers and blooming gardens. The weather remains mild, making it ideal for leisurely walks along the cliffside paths or relaxing on the tranquil beaches. Moreover, this shoulder season allows you to avoid the overwhelming crowds that flock to Santorini during the peak summer months.

Summer (June to August) is undoubtedly the high season for Santorini tourism. The island experiences scorching temperatures, attracting sun-seekers from around the world. The allure of breathtaking sunsets and vibrant nightlife comes alive during these months. However, be prepared for larger crowds, higher prices, and the need to book accommodations well in advance.

If you prefer a more laid-back and serene experience, consider visiting Santorini during the fall (September to October). The weather remains pleasant, and the sea is still warm enough for swimming. As the number of visitors starts to dwindle, you can better savor the island's charm and immerse yourself in its authentic culture.

Winter (November to March) offers a unique perspective of Santorini. While some facilities and attractions may close during this period, you'll find tranquility and the opportunity to engage with the locals on a deeper level. The weather might be cooler, but the island's charm endures, and you can enjoy lower prices on accommodations and flights.

Ultimately, the best time to visit Santorini depends on what you value most in your travel experience. Whether you seek lively summer nights, vibrant spring blossoms, or a peaceful escape in the off-season, Santorini awaits with its captivating beauty and everlasting allure.

Chapter 2. Planning Your Trip

2.1 Visa and Travel Requirements

Santorini is a stunning island in the Cyclades archipelago of Greece, known for its breathtaking sunsets, white-washed buildings, and crystal-clear waters. Traveling to Santorini involves considering visa requirements, entry regulations, and other essential travel details.

Visa Requirements:
Greece, including Santorini, is a part of the Schengen Area, which allows for seamless travel between its member countries. Depending on your nationality, you might need a Schengen visa to enter Santorini. Citizens of many countries, including the United States, Canada, Australia, and most European Union nations, can enter Greece for tourism purposes without a visa and stay for up to 90 days within a 180-day period. However, travelers from some countries may need to apply for a Schengen visa in advance.

Travel Documents:
Ensure you have a valid passport that will remain valid for at least three months beyond your intended departure date from Santorini. It's wise to

have a copy of your passport and other important documents stored separately in case of loss or theft.

Entry Regulations:
When you arrive in Santorini, you will need to go through immigration and customs procedures. Be prepared to provide necessary information such as the purpose of your visit, proof of accommodation (hotel reservations), return flight details, and sufficient funds to cover your stay. Travelers may also be asked to provide evidence of travel insurance.

Health and Safety:
Travellers to Santorini are advised to have comprehensive travel insurance that covers medical expenses and repatriation. The island's medical facilities are generally of good quality, but having insurance can provide peace of mind.

In summary, visiting Santorini requires travelers to have a valid passport, possibly a Schengen visa depending on nationality, proof of accommodation, return flight details, and sufficient funds.

2.2 Getting to Santorini

Getting to Santorini, the picturesque Greek island known for its stunning sunsets, white-washed buildings, and crystal-clear waters, is an exciting and rewarding journey. Whether you're travelling internationally or within Europe, there are several options available to reach this enchanting destination.

1. Flights: Santorini has its own international airport, Santorini Thira Airport (JTR), which receives direct flights from various European cities and major international hubs. During peak travel seasons, airlines often increase the frequency of flights to accommodate the influx of tourists. Flight durations can vary depending on your departure location, with shorter flights available from neighbouring countries such as Greece, Italy, and Turkey.

2. Ferries: If you prefer a more scenic route, taking a ferry to Santorini is a popular choice. The island is well-connected by ferry services from Athens' major ports (Piraeus and Rafina), as well as other nearby islands. The journey can range from a few hours to overnight, depending on the departure point and type of ferry. High-speed catamarans and slower, more spacious conventional ferries are available options.

3. Cruises: Santorini is a favourite port of call for many Mediterranean cruise itineraries. Arriving by cruise ship allows you to enjoy a glimpse of the island's beauty and charm within a limited time. Cruise passengers are often tendered from the ship to Santorini's port, Athinios, where they can explore the island or take organized excursions.

4. Domestic Flights: If you're already in Greece, you can take domestic flights from Athens or other major cities to Santorini. This option offers convenience and can significantly reduce travel time compared to ferries.

5. Transfers: Once you arrive in Santorini, you can easily reach your accommodations using various transportation options. Taxis, rental cars, and shuttle services are readily available at the airport and port. Additionally, many hotels offer transfer services to ensure a smooth arrival experience.

It's important to plan your trip to Santorini well in advance, especially during the peak travel months of June to September. Flight and ferry tickets, as well as accommodations, tend to get booked quickly during this period. Weather conditions can also affect ferry schedules, so it's advisable to check for updates before traveling.

In conclusion, getting to Santorini offers a range of transportation choices, each providing its own unique experience. Whether you prefer the convenience of flying or the leisurely pace of a ferry ride, reaching this idyllic island is the first step toward creating unforgettable memories in one of the most iconic destinations in the world.

2.3 Transportation on the Island

Transportation on the island of Santorini primarily relies on a few key modes of transportation due to its unique geography and stunning landscapes. The island's transportation network is designed to accommodate the influx of tourists and residents while preserving the beauty of its surroundings.

1. Buses: Santorini has a well-developed bus network that connects its major towns, villages, and popular attractions. Buses are a cost-effective and convenient way to explore the island. They offer air-conditioned comfort and usually run on time, making them a popular choice for both tourists and locals.

2. Taxis: Taxis are readily available and provide a more personalized mode of transportation. They are particularly useful for reaching destinations not

covered by the bus routes or for private tours. However, taxis can be relatively more expensive compared to buses.

3. Rental Cars and ATVs: Many tourists opt to rent cars, scooters, or all-terrain vehicles (ATVs) to explore Santorini at their own pace. While this offers flexibility and access to more remote areas, it's important to note that the island's roads can be narrow and winding, especially in some villages. Caution is advised, and an international driver's license may be required.

4. Cable Car and Donkeys: One of the most iconic transportation experiences in Santorini is the cable car that connects the Old Port (Skala) with the town of Fira. Alternatively, visitors can choose to ride traditional donkeys up the steep cliffside. These options offer a unique and memorable way to access Fira from the port, but they can get crowded during peak tourist seasons.

5. Walking: Exploring Santorini on foot is a fantastic way to soak in the island's breathtaking views, architecture, and natural beauty. While it may not be feasible to walk long distances between towns due to the island's topography, strolling

within towns and enjoying leisurely walks along caldera pathways is a popular pastime.

6. Boat Tours: Given Santorini's volcanic nature and caldera, boat tours are a popular activity. These tours offer the chance to explore nearby islands, swim in hot springs, and witness the famous sunset from the water. Boat tours provide a different perspective of Santorini's landscape and are a must-do for many visitors.

7. Cycling: Cycling enthusiasts can rent bicycles to explore the island's scenic routes, especially in areas with less traffic. Some accommodations offer bike rentals, and cycling allows for a slower-paced, eco-friendly exploration of Santorini.

It's important to note that Santorini experiences a significant influx of tourists, especially during the peak summer months. This can result in crowded transportation options, so planning ahead and considering off-peak hours can enhance the overall experience. Additionally, transportation availability and options may vary due to local regulations, weather conditions, and changes in tourism trends.

Chapter 3. Top Attractions

3.1 Oia Village

Oia (pronounced "ee-ah") is a picturesque village located on the northwest tip of the Greek island of Santorini. Renowned for its stunning sunsets, white-washed buildings, and panoramic views of the Aegean Sea, Oia is a popular tourist destination and has become synonymous with the postcard-perfect image of Santorini.

The architecture of Oia is characterized by its distinctive Cycladic design, featuring traditional cube-shaped houses carved into the cliffs. These whitewashed buildings are accentuated by blue-domed churches, narrow cobblestone streets, and charming alleyways that wind through the village. The design not only adds to the village's unique charm but also helps to keep the interiors cool during the hot summer months.

One of the main draws of Oia is its breathtaking sunsets. The village offers numerous vantage points from which visitors can watch the sun dip below the horizon, casting a golden glow over the caldera and creating a magical atmosphere. The sunset viewpoint at the Oia Castle, also known as the

Byzantine Castle Ruins, is particularly famous for providing an unforgettable sunset experience.

Oia is also known for its vibrant art scene, with many galleries showcasing local and international artists. Visitors can explore art studios and galleries displaying a wide range of works, from traditional paintings to contemporary sculptures and crafts.

Culinary experiences in Oia are equally captivating. The village boasts an array of restaurants and tavernas serving both traditional Greek cuisine and international dishes. Seafood is a highlight, and visitors can enjoy freshly caught fish while savoring the stunning views of the caldera and the sea.

Accommodation options in Oia range from luxury boutique hotels to charming guesthouses, many of which offer breathtaking views and an intimate atmosphere. Staying in Oia provides an opportunity to immerse oneself in the village's romantic ambiance and unique architecture.

However, Oia's popularity also means that it can become quite crowded during peak tourist seasons, especially around sunset. Travelers looking to avoid the crowds might consider visiting during the shoulder seasons of spring and fall, when the weather is still pleasant, and the atmosphere is more relaxed.

In essence, Oia Village in Santorini is a captivating destination that captures the essence of Greek island beauty, with its iconic architecture, mesmerizing sunsets, artistic allure, and culinary delights. It remains a place that continues to captivate the hearts of travelers seeking a truly enchanting experience on this enchanting island.

3.2 Fira Town

Fira Town, often referred to simply as Fira, is the vibrant capital of the picturesque Greek island of Santorini. Situated on the western coast of the island, Fira is renowned for its stunning views, white-washed buildings, and charming ambiance. Here's an overview of Fira Town:

1. Location and Geography: Fira is perched on the edge of the caldera, a crescent-shaped volcanic crater formed by a massive volcanic eruption thousands of years ago. This unique geographic setting provides visitors with breathtaking panoramic views of the Aegean Sea, the surrounding islands, and the iconic Santorini sunsets.

2. Architecture and Aesthetics: The traditional Cycladic architecture of Fira is characterized by its white-washed buildings with blue-domed roofs and narrow cobblestone streets. This distinctive architectural style is not only visually striking but also serves practical purposes, such as reflecting sunlight and efficiently utilizing space in the town's layout.

3. Cultural Attractions: Fira offers a variety of cultural attractions, including museums, galleries, and historical sites. The Museum of Prehistoric Thera showcases artifacts from the ancient Minoan settlement of Akrotiri, which was buried under volcanic ash. Visitors can also explore the Orthodox Metropolitan Cathedral, built in the 19th century, and the Catholic Cathedral.

4. Shopping and Dining: Fira boasts a wide range of shops, boutiques, and artisanal studios where visitors can find local crafts, jewellery, textiles, and souvenirs. The town's vibrant dining scene offers a mix of traditional Greek tavernas, seafood restaurants, and international cuisine, providing an array of culinary options for all tastes.

5. Nightlife and Entertainment: As the capital of Santorini, Fira offers a lively nightlife scene with

bars, clubs, and live music venues. Many establishments stay open late, making Fira a popular destination for those seeking evening entertainment and socializing.

6. Transportation: Fira serves as a transportation hub on Santorini, connecting visitors to other parts of the island. The town has a bus terminal with routes to various villages and beaches, as well as a cable car that provides a quick and scenic ride down to the Old Port. Donkey rides and hiking are alternative ways to reach the port.

7. Accommodation: Fira offers a range of accommodation options, from luxury hotels with stunning caldera views to charming boutique guesthouses and budget-friendly hostels. The town's central location makes it a convenient base for exploring other parts of Santorini.

8. Festivals and Events: Throughout the year, Fira hosts various cultural and religious festivals, including traditional Greek celebrations, music festivals, and art exhibitions. These events provide visitors with the opportunity to experience the local culture and community.

9. Outdoor Activities: Beyond its cultural attractions, Fira also offers outdoor activities such as hiking along scenic trails, exploring the volcanic landscape, and enjoying boat tours around the caldera. Adventurous travelers can even take part in water sports, including snorkelling, diving, and swimming.

In summary, Fira Town in Santorini is a captivating destination that encapsulates the charm and beauty of the Cycladic islands. With its stunning vistas, cultural richness, and vibrant atmosphere, Fira offers a unique and memorable experience for travelers from around the world.

3.3 Akrotiri Archaeological Site

The Akrotiri Archaeological Site is a captivating historical treasure located on the Greek island of Santorini. Often referred to as the "Pompeii of the Aegean," this site offers a remarkable glimpse into an ancient civilization that was buried under layers of volcanic ash and pumice following the massive eruption of the Thera volcano around 1600 BCE.

The settlement of Akrotiri dates back to the Late Neolithic period, but it reached its peak during the Bronze Age. The site was a thriving Minoan trading and maritime hub, characterized by advanced urban planning, multi-story buildings, intricate frescoes, and a sophisticated drainage system. The architecture and artifacts found at Akrotiri provide valuable insights into the daily life, culture, and technological achievements of the Minoans.

The eruption of Thera in the mid-second millennium BCE was catastrophic, burying the entire settlement under thick layers of volcanic debris. However, this natural disaster also preserved the site remarkably well, much like Pompeii in Italy. Excavations, which began in the late 1960s, have uncovered a wealth of artifacts and structures, including pottery, pottery, tools, furniture, and elaborate wall paintings depicting scenes of daily life, religious rituals, and the natural world.

The Akrotiri Archaeological Site has greatly contributed to our understanding of the ancient Aegean civilizations, shedding light on their trade networks, artistic achievements, and technological advancements. The preserved buildings and artifacts offer clues about the society's economic activities, social hierarchy, and cultural practices.

Visitors to the site can explore the well-preserved streets, houses, and public spaces, gaining a vivid sense of what life was like in this ancient city. The site also features an impressive wooden roof structure that protects the archaeological remains from the elements while allowing visitors to experience the unique atmosphere of Akrotiri.

In recent years, efforts have been made to improve the site's preservation and presentation, enhancing the visitor experience. The Akrotiri Archaeological Site stands as a testament to the resilience of ancient civilizations and their ability to adapt to and thrive in challenging environments, as well as a remarkable window into the past that continues to captivate and educate visitors from around the world.

3.4 Red Beach

Red Beach, located on the stunning Greek island of Santorini, is a unique and captivating natural wonder renowned for its striking crimson-hued sand and dramatic cliffs. This picturesque destination is a popular stop for visitors seeking a one-of-a-kind beach experience in the Aegean Sea.

The mesmerizing red color of the beach's sand is attributed to the presence of iron-rich minerals and volcanic activity. Over the years, volcanic eruptions and geological processes have shaped the landscape, resulting in the distinctive reddish hue that sets Red Beach apart from other beaches around the world. The intense contrast between the deep blue waters of the sea and the vibrant red sand creates a visual spectacle that draws in photographers, nature enthusiasts, and travelers alike.

To access Red Beach, visitors typically embark on a short hike from the nearby village of Akrotiri. The path winds through rugged terrain and along cliffside trails, providing breathtaking panoramic views of the surrounding landscape and the Aegean Sea. Upon reaching the beach, visitors are greeted by a small cove surrounded by towering red cliffs, creating a secluded and intimate atmosphere.

While the beach's unique appearance is its main draw, the underwater world of Red Beach also offers excellent opportunities for snorkeling and swimming. The crystal-clear waters allow visitors to observe a variety of marine life and colorful underwater formations, adding to the allure of the destination.

It's important to note that due to the beach's popularity and the potential for landslides from the surrounding cliffs, there are safety precautions in place, and visitors are advised to be cautious while exploring the area. Accessibility and safety measures may have evolved, so I recommend checking with local authorities or recent travel guides for the most up-to-date information before planning a visit.

In conclusion, Red Beach in Santorini is a captivating testament to the forces of nature, offering a truly unique and awe-inspiring beach experience. Its iconic red sand, dramatic cliffs, and clear blue waters combine to create an enchanting destination that continues to leave a lasting impression on those fortunate enough to experience its beauty.

3.5 Perissa and Kamari Beaches

Perissa and Kamari are two popular beaches located on the island of Santorini in Greece. Known for their stunning black volcanic sand and crystal-clear blue waters, these beaches offer a unique and picturesque setting for visitors to enjoy. Here's an overview of both beaches:

Perissa Beach:
Perissa Beach is situated on the southeastern coast of Santorini and is famous for its distinctive black sand, a result of the island's volcanic history. The

beach stretches for about 7 kilometres and is surrounded by dramatic cliffs, creating a breathtaking backdrop. Perissa is known for its relaxed and vibrant atmosphere, making it a favorite among both locals and tourists.

Features and Activities at Perissa Beach:
- Water Sports: Perissa offers various water sports activities such as jet skiing, paddleboarding, and kayaking, making it a hub of adventure for water enthusiasts.
- Beach Bars and Restaurants: The beach is lined with beach bars and restaurants offering a wide range of cuisine, from traditional Greek dishes to international flavors.
- Accommodation: Perissa has a range of accommodation options, including hotels, resorts, and guesthouses, allowing visitors to stay close to the beach.
- Ancient Thera: At the end of Perissa Beach, there's a path leading to Ancient Thera, an archaeological site with ruins dating back to the Hellenistic, Roman, and Byzantine periods. The hike provides stunning views of the surrounding area.

Kamari Beach:
Kamari Beach is located on the eastern coast of Santorini and, like Perissa, features black volcanic

sand and clear waters. It's a well-organised beach with a promenade lined with shops, cafes, and restaurants, creating a lively and convenient atmosphere for visitors.

Features and Activities at Kamari Beach:
- Waterfront Promenade: Kamari's promenade is a bustling area where visitors can find a wide range of shops selling clothing, jewellery, souvenirs, and more. There are also numerous restaurants and cafes along the promenade.
- Open-Air Cinema: Kamari boasts a unique open-air cinema where visitors can enjoy a movie under the stars while sitting on comfortable loungers.
- Water Activities: Like Perissa, Kamari offers various water sports activities, providing entertainment for those looking to engage in active pursuits.
- Archaeological Sites: Nearby, you can find the Ancient Thera archaeological site accessible via a hiking path, much like at Perissa Beach.

Both Perissa and Kamari beaches offer a blend of natural beauty, recreational activities, and cultural experiences. Whether you're interested in lounging by the sea, exploring ancient ruins, enjoying water sports, or indulging in local cuisine, these beaches have something to offer for everyone visiting Santorini.

3.6 Ancient Thera

Ancient Thera, also known as Thera or Thira, is an archaeological site located on the Greek island of Santorini (officially known as Thira). This site offers a fascinating glimpse into the history of the region, showcasing the remnants of a once-thriving ancient city that played a significant role in the Mediterranean world.

Historical Background:
Ancient Thera was inhabited from the 9th century BC until around 726 AD when it was abandoned due to a volcanic eruption. This eruption, known as the Minoan eruption, is often associated with the decline of the Minoan civilization and may have inspired the myth of Atlantis due to its catastrophic impact on the Aegean region.

Archaeological Significance:
The archaeological site of Ancient Thera is perched on the steep slopes of Mesa Vouno, a mountain in Santorini. The site provides valuable insights into the lives of its inhabitants and their interactions with other ancient civilizations. The excavations at Ancient Thera have uncovered ruins of houses,

streets, temples, and various structures, revealing the layout and architectural styles of the ancient city.

Key Features:
1. Agora and Temples: The site features a central agora (public square) surrounded by several temples dedicated to various deities, including Apollo, Artemis, and Dionysus. These religious structures provide insights into the spiritual practices of the ancient Theraeans.

2. Residential Buildings: The remains of houses with multiple rooms, courtyards, and indoor plumbing systems showcase the daily life of the city's inhabitants. The design of these houses reflects the architectural trends of the time.

3. Gymnasium and Theater: Ancient Thera also boasts a gymnasium and a small theatre, highlighting the importance of physical and cultural activities in the lives of its residents.

4. Cemetery: A necropolis containing tombs and funerary monuments sheds light on ancient burial practices and societal beliefs surrounding death.

5. Trade and Connectivity: The location of Ancient Thera on a prominent hill overlooking the Aegean Sea indicates its strategic importance in trade and maritime activities. The city likely played a role in connecting the Aegean world with other civilizations in the Mediterranean.

Visiting Ancient Thera:
Today, visitors can explore the archaeological site of Ancient Thera and witness the well-preserved remnants of this ancient city. The site can be reached via a challenging hike or by car from Kamari, a nearby town. The panoramic views of the surrounding landscape and the Aegean Sea add to the allure of the visit.

Conclusion:
Ancient Thera stands as a testament to the enduring legacy of civilizations that once thrived in the Aegean region. Its archaeological significance, historical context, and stunning location make it a captivating destination for history enthusiasts, archaeologists, and travelers interested in uncovering the mysteries of the past.

Chapter 4. Activities and Experiences

4.1 Sunset Cruises

Sunset cruises in Santorini offer a captivating and enchanting experience that allows visitors to witness the island's iconic sunsets from a unique perspective. Santorini, a stunning Greek island renowned for its white-washed buildings, crystal-clear waters, and breathtaking caldera views, becomes even more magical when viewed from the deck of a boat during the sunset hours.

These cruises typically embark from the picturesque town of Oia or the Old Port in Fira, the island's capital. The catamarans or traditional wooden boats used for these cruises provide a comfortable and luxurious setting for passengers to enjoy the scenic beauty around them. The cruise route often takes passengers along the rugged coastline, passing by iconic landmarks such as the Red Beach, White Beach, and the volcanic islands within the caldera.

As the sun begins its descent towards the horizon, the true magic of the sunset cruise unfolds. The play of colors across the sky—shades of orange, pink, and purple—creates a mesmerizing backdrop against the stunning backdrop of Santorini's cliffs and traditional architecture. Passengers have the opportunity to capture incredible photographs and enjoy uninterrupted views as the sun dips below the Aegean Sea.

Many sunset cruises also offer onboard amenities, including gourmet meals featuring local cuisine, refreshing beverages, and a relaxed atmosphere. Some cruises even include opportunities for swimming or snorkeling in the crystal-clear waters of the caldera. The combination of the tranquil sea, the stunning natural beauty, and the warm hues of the sunset create an unforgettable ambiance that makes these cruises a top choice for honeymooners, couples, and travelers seeking a romantic and idyllic experience.

It's worth noting that Santorini is a popular tourist destination, and sunset cruises can get fully booked, especially during peak travel seasons. It's advisable to book your cruise in advance to secure your spot and ensure that you can enjoy this unique and enchanting experience. Whether you're looking for a romantic getaway, a memorable honeymoon, or simply a serene way to soak in Santorini's beauty, a sunset cruise is a must-do activity that will leave you with lasting memories of this stunning Greek island.

4.2 Winery Tours

Winery tours in Santorini offer a captivating experience that combines the island's stunning landscapes with its rich wine-making heritage. Located in the Aegean Sea, Santorini is renowned for its unique vineyards cultivated in volcanic soil, resulting in distinctive and flavorful wines. Here's an overview of winery tours on this enchanting Greek island:

1. Scenic Vineyards: Santorini's dramatic terrain features terraced vineyards that cling to the island's caldera cliffs. The panoramic views of the Aegean Sea and neighboring islands provide an awe-inspiring backdrop for your winery tour.

2. Indigenous Grape Varieties: The island boasts indigenous grape varieties, notably Assyrtiko, Athiri, and Aidani. These grapes thrive in the volcanic soil, producing wines with exceptional character, minerality, and acidity.

3. Wine-Making Process: During the tour, you'll have the chance to witness the wine-making process firsthand. Guides explain the grape harvest, traditional stomping methods, and modern techniques used in wine production.

4. Tasting Sessions: Winery tours typically culminate in tasting sessions where you can savour a variety of wines, including whites, reds, and dessert wines. These tastings often include Assyrtiko, the flagship grape, known for its crispness and versatility.

5. Wine Cellars: Santorini's wineries often feature charming cellars where wines are aged and stored. The cool, dimly lit atmosphere adds to the allure of the tasting experience.

6. Food Pairing: Many winery tours incorporate delectable food pairings, showcasing local cuisine that complements the wines perfectly. You can enjoy dishes such as fresh seafood, cheeses, olives, and traditional Greek delicacies.

7. Educational Experience: Guided tours offer insights into the island's winemaking traditions, history, and the challenges posed by its unique climate. Learn about the impact of volcanic soil, strong winds, and limited rainfall on grape cultivation.

8. Sunset Tours: Santorini is renowned for its breathtaking sunsets. Some wineries offer sunset tours, allowing you to enjoy the stunning vistas

while sipping on local wines. These tours often require advance booking due to high demand.

9. Local Wineries: Several notable wineries in Santorini offer exceptional tour experiences. Some of the renowned ones include Santo Wines, Venetsanos Winery, Gaia Wines, and Domaine Sigalas.

10. Cultural Immersion: Beyond the wines, winery tours provide a glimpse into the island's culture and way of life. Engage with local winemakers and staff to gain insights into the island's past and present.

11. Souvenirs and Gifts: Most wineries have onsite shops where you can purchase bottles of your favourite wines as well as wine-related accessories and souvenirs to commemorate your visit.

In summary, winery tours in Santorini are an enchanting blend of natural beauty, cultural exploration, and the appreciation of exceptional wines. The combination of unique grape varieties, volcanic soil, and stunning landscapes make these tours a must-do experience for visitors seeking to immerse themselves in the island's rich wine-making heritage.

4.3 Hiking Trails

Santorini, renowned for its stunning sunsets, white-washed buildings, and crystal-clear waters, might not be the first place that comes to mind when thinking of hiking trails. However, this picturesque Greek island offers a surprising array of trails that allow visitors to experience its natural beauty beyond the typical tourist spots.

1. Fira to Oia Trail: Arguably the most famous trail on the island, this roughly 10-kilometer (6-mile) path connects the capital, Fira, to the charming village of Oia. The trail offers breathtaking views of the caldera, the Aegean Sea, and the iconic blue-domed churches. The best time to embark on this hike is either early morning or late afternoon to avoid the heat of the day.

2. Ancient Thira Trail: For history enthusiasts, the Ancient Thira Trail is a must. This hike takes you up to the ruins of Ancient Thira, an ancient city dating back to the 9th century BC. Along the way, you'll be treated to panoramic views of Kamari Beach and the surrounding coastline.

3. Pyrgos to Profitis Ilias Trail: This trail leads from the charming village of Pyrgos to the highest point on the island, Profitis Ilias. The hike takes you

through quaint villages, vineyards, and offers sweeping views of Santorini's unique landscape. Once you reach the summit, you'll be rewarded with a panoramic vista that stretches across the entire island.

4. Perissa to Ancient Thira Trail: Starting from the black sand beach of Perissa, this trail takes you to the ruins of Ancient Thira. Along the way, you'll pass through diverse terrain, including rocky paths and lush valleys, providing a unique perspective of Santorini's geological features.

5. Akrotiri Lighthouse Trail: This relatively easy hike leads to the Akrotiri Lighthouse at the southern tip of the island. The trail offers stunning views of the rugged coastline, the deep blue sea, and the caldera cliffs. It's an ideal spot for watching the sunset away from the crowds.

6. Mesa Vouno Trail: Mesa Vouno is the site of an ancient city and is often referred to as the "Santorini Pompeii." The hike to Mesa Vouno provides an opportunity to explore archaeological remains while taking in panoramic views of Kamari Beach and the surrounding area.

7. Vlychada to Fira Trail: Starting from the Vlychada Marina, this trail leads you through lunar-like landscapes, showcasing the island's unique geological formations. The route takes you through the heart of Santorini, passing by villages and offering glimpses of local life.

It's important to note that Santorini's hiking trails can vary in difficulty and length, so it's recommended to check the specific trail details and conditions before embarking on any hike. Additionally, as the weather can be quite hot during the summer months, it's advisable to bring plenty of water, wear appropriate footwear, and protect yourself from the sun.

Exploring Santorini's hiking trails not only allows you to connect with its natural beauty but also offers a different perspective on the island's history, culture, and breathtaking landscapes.

4.4 Water Sports and Beach Activities

Santorini, a stunning Greek island renowned for its captivating beauty, offers a plethora of water sports and beach activities that cater to every type of traveler. Whether you seek adrenaline-pumping adventures or tranquil relaxation, Santorini's crystal-clear waters and idyllic beaches provide the perfect backdrop for a memorable vacation.

1. Swimming and Sunbathing: The island boasts numerous beaches, each with its own unique charm. The most famous are Perissa and Kamari, known for their black sand, and Red Beach, named after its distinctive reddish volcanic sand. Spend your days basking in the Mediterranean sun and taking refreshing dips in the turquoise waters.

2. Snorkelling and Scuba Diving: Santorini's underwater world is a playground for snorkelers and divers. Explore vibrant marine life, underwater caves, and submerged volcanic formations. The volcanic caldera offers intriguing dive sites with submerged craters, lava formations, and a rich diversity of marine species.

3. Kayaking and Paddleboarding: Navigate the island's captivating coastline by kayaking or paddleboarding. Paddle through hidden sea caves and marvel at the stunning cliffs, creating an intimate connection with the island's natural beauty.

4. Jet Skiing and Water Skiing: Thrill-seekers can indulge in jet skiing and water skiing, speeding

across the azure waters with a backdrop of dramatic cliffs and picturesque villages.

5. Sailing and Catamaran Tours: Experience Santorini from a different perspective by embarking on a sailing or catamaran tour. Cruise along the caldera, witness breathtaking sunsets, and visit nearby islets for a day of relaxation and exploration.

6. Windsurfing and Kitesurfing: The island's consistent wind patterns make it an ideal destination for windsurfing and kitesurfing enthusiasts. Head to beaches like Vlychada or Avis for thrilling water sports experiences.

7. Parasailing: Soar above the coastline and enjoy panoramic views of Santorini's rugged cliffs and pristine waters while parasailing. This activity offers an unforgettable perspective of the island's beauty.

8. Beach Volleyball and Beach Soccer: Many of Santorini's beaches have designated areas for beach volleyball and beach soccer, allowing visitors to engage in friendly competitions while enjoying the sun and sand.

9. Fishing Trips: Embark on a fishing excursion and discover the art of traditional Greek fishing. Whether you're a seasoned angler or a novice, the experienced local fishermen will guide you through the process.

10. Relaxation and Yoga: For those seeking a more serene experience, Santorini offers beachfront yoga sessions and meditation classes. Immerse yourself in the tranquil surroundings while finding inner peace and rejuvenation.

As you indulge in these water sports and beach activities, remember to prioritize safety by adhering to local guidelines and regulations. Whether you're an adventure enthusiast or a relaxation seeker, Santorini's diverse offerings ensure a memorable and fulfilling vacation experience.

Chapter 5. Where to Stay

5.1 Luxury Resorts

Santorini, a picturesque Greek island in the Aegean Sea, is renowned for its breathtaking sunsets, azure waters, and stunning landscapes. The island's luxury resorts offer an unparalleled blend of opulence, comfort, and mesmerizing views, making Santorini a dream destination for travellers seeking an unforgettable getaway.

1. Astarte Suites: Nestled atop a cliff overlooking the Caldera, Astarte Suites is a gem of luxury. With private plunge pools, elegant suites, and personalized service, guests are treated to a romantic and serene atmosphere. The resort's exquisite design, inspired by Cycladic architecture, seamlessly integrates with the island's natural beauty.

2. Grace Santorini: Perched on the hills of Imerovigli, Grace Santorini boasts minimalist elegance and awe-inspiring vistas. Its infinity pool seems to blend with the sea, creating an illusion of endless horizons. Gourmet dining, exceptional spa treatments, and luxurious accommodations make Grace Santorini a haven of indulgence.

3. Canaves Oia Suites: Located in the iconic village of Oia, Canaves Oia Suites offers sumptuous suites carved into the cliffs. With whitewashed walls, domed ceilings, and private verandas featuring mesmerising sea views, guests experience the quintessential Santorini charm. The resort's Michelin-starred restaurant, La Table, ensures a culinary experience of the highest calibre.

4. Mystique, a Luxury Collection Hotel: Mystique transports visitors to a world of enchantment with its cave-style suites and a blend of modern amenities and traditional aesthetics. Its open-air cinema, dramatic infinity pool, and sea-facing terraces provide an intimate connection to Santorini's natural beauty.

5. Santo Maris Oia Luxury Suites & Spa: Offering a blend of luxury and authentic Greek hospitality, Santo Maris showcases elegant suites, private pools, and a holistic spa. Guests can savour culinary delights at Alios Ilios restaurant or indulge in a sunset cruise aboard the resort's private yacht.

6. Katikies Hotel: With a collection of luxurious suites and villas, Katikies Hotel presents captivating Caldera views and impeccable service. Each room is a testament to the island's charm, featuring pristine

white interiors, private balconies, and romantic alcoves.

7. Perivolas Hotel: Transformed from 300-year-old caves, Perivolas Hotel combines rustic charm with contemporary luxury. Its infinity pool and spa terraces cascade down the cliffside, offering a serene space to unwind. Guests are treated to personalized services, including private dining experiences and yacht charters.

8. Andronis Luxury Suites: Situated in Oia's romantic setting, Andronis Luxury Suites showcases elegantly designed suites with indoor plunge pools and spellbinding views. The resort's multi-level infinity pool and world-class dining ensure an indulgent experience.

9. Vedema, a Luxury Collection Resort: Nestled in the quaint village of Megalochori, Vedema offers a different Santorini experience with its vineyard setting and traditional architecture. The resort features spacious villas, a historic 400-year-old winery, and exclusive wine tastings.

10. Cavo Tagoo Santorini: A blend of modern design and island charm, Cavo Tagoo offers luxurious suites with private plunge pools and

panoramic sea views. The resort's spa, fitness centre, and trendy poolside bar create a vibrant atmosphere for relaxation and enjoyment.

In conclusion, luxury resorts in Santorini elevate the concept of opulent travel to new heights. With their awe-inspiring locations, lavish accommodations, and top-notch amenities, these resorts provide an unparalleled experience of indulgence and relaxation against the backdrop of one of the most captivating islands in the world.

5.2 Boutique Hotels

Boutique hotels in Santorini offer a unique and luxurious experience for travelers seeking an intimate and personalised stay on this picturesque Greek island. Known for its stunning sunsets, crystal-clear waters, and charming white-washed buildings, Santorini serves as an ideal backdrop for these distinctive accommodations.

1. Characteristics of Boutique Hotels in Santorini:
   Boutique hotels are characterised by their small size, attention to detail, and distinctive design. In Santorini, these properties often feature traditional Cycladic architecture with a modern twist. Expect minimalistic aesthetics, local artwork, and carefully curated interiors that reflect the island's culture and

natural beauty. Many boutique hotels boast panoramic views of the Aegean Sea, providing guests with an unforgettable setting.

2. Unique Accommodations:

Santorini's boutique hotels offer a variety of accommodation options, from cozy rooms to lavish suites. Some properties feature cave-like dwellings carved into the cliffs, creating a sense of seclusion and intimacy. Private balconies, plunge pools, and jacuzzis are common amenities, providing guests with the opportunity to relax and soak in the island's ambiance.

3. Personalised Service:

One of the hallmarks of boutique hotels is their exceptional service. With a smaller number of rooms, staff can provide more personalized attention to each guest. From arranging private tours and transportation to recommending local dining spots, these hotels strive to create a tailored experience that caters to individual preferences.

4. Culinary Delights:

Many boutique hotels in Santorini pride themselves on their culinary offerings. Guests can enjoy authentic Greek cuisine prepared with locally sourced ingredients. Some properties feature on-site restaurants and bars with breathtaking views, adding to the overall dining experience.

5. Wellness and Relaxation:
Several boutique hotels emphasise wellness and relaxation, offering spa services, yoga classes, and wellness programs. These amenities complement the tranquil atmosphere of Santorini, allowing guests to rejuvenate both their bodies and minds.

6. Romantic Getaways:
The romantic ambiance of Santorini makes it a popular destination for couples, and boutique hotels often cater to honeymooners and those celebrating special occasions. Intimate settings, luxurious amenities, and romantic packages contribute to the island's reputation as a dreamy getaway.

7. Local Experiences:
Boutique hotels in Santorini often collaborate with local artisans and businesses, offering guests the opportunity to immerse themselves in the island's culture. Wine tastings, cooking classes, and guided tours can provide a deeper understanding of Santorini's rich heritage.

8. Sustainability and Eco-Friendly Practices:

Many boutique hotels in Santorini prioritise sustainability and eco-friendly practices. From using local and organic products to implementing energy-saving initiatives, these properties aim to minimise their environmental impact while providing a high-end experience.

In conclusion, boutique hotels in Santorini offer a blend of luxury, personalized service, and authentic experiences against the backdrop of one of the world's most captivating destinations. Whether you're seeking a romantic escape, a wellness retreat, or simply a unique and unforgettable getaway, these accommodations provide an ideal haven for travelers looking to indulge in the beauty and charm of Santorini.

5.3 Budget-Friendly Accommodations

Finding budget-friendly accommodations in Santorini requires some research and planning, as the island is known for its luxurious and picturesque hotels. However, there are still ways to enjoy this stunning destination without breaking the bank. Here are some tips for budget-friendly accommodations in Santorini:

1. Off-Peak Travel: Consider visiting Santorini during the shoulder seasons, which are spring

(April to early June) and fall (September to October). Accommodation prices are generally lower during these times compared to the peak summer months.

2. Booking in Advance: Secure your accommodations well in advance to take advantage of early booking discounts and to ensure availability at budget-friendly options.

3. Stay in Fira or Kamari: While the iconic Caldera views in Oia and Imerovigli are breathtaking, staying in towns like Fira or Kamari can be more budget-friendly. These areas offer a variety of accommodation options, including hostels, guesthouses, and small hotels.

4. Hostels and Guesthouses: Look for hostels or guesthouses, as they tend to offer more affordable rates compared to larger hotels. Many of these options still provide comfortable and clean lodgings.

5. Local Rentals and Apartments: Consider renting a local apartment or studio through platforms like Airbnb or Booking.com. This option can be more cost-effective, especially if you're travelling with a group and can split the costs.

6. Search for Deals: Utilise hotel and travel booking websites to search for deals, discounts, and special offers on accommodations. Sometimes, you can find package deals that include accommodations and other perks.

7. Avoid All-Inclusive Resorts: While all-inclusive resorts may seem convenient, they can often be pricier. Instead, opt for accommodations that offer basic amenities and explore local dining options to save on food expenses.

8. Local Pensions and Family-Run Inns: Look for family-run inns and local pensions, which can provide a more authentic experience and may be more budget-friendly compared to larger, chain hotels.

9. Shared Accommodations: If you're open to it, consider shared accommodations where you book a room in a shared apartment or villa. This can significantly reduce costs.

10. Check for Added Amenities: Some budget accommodations might offer extras like a kitchenette, allowing you to prepare simple meals and save on dining expenses.

11. Use Public Transportation: Opt for accommodations near public transportation options to easily explore the island without the need for expensive car rentals.

12. Flexibility in Travel Dates: If your travel dates are flexible, you might be able to find better deals by adjusting your itinerary based on the availability of budget-friendly accommodations.

13. Negotiate Directly: In some cases, you might be able to negotiate directly with the accommodation provider for a better rate, especially if you're booking for an extended stay.

Remember that while budget-friendly options can help you save money, it's important to read reviews and do your research to ensure that the accommodations meet your basic comfort and cleanliness standards. By being strategic and considering these tips, you can enjoy the beauty of Santorini without overspending on accommodations.

Chapter 6. Dining and Cuisine

6.1 Traditional Greek Restaurants

Santorini, a picturesque island in the Aegean Sea, is renowned for its breathtaking sunsets, stunning landscapes, and rich cultural heritage. Traditional Greek restaurants on this enchanting island offer an authentic culinary experience that reflects the island's history, culture, and flavours.

1. Ambiance and Atmosphere: Traditional Greek restaurants in Santorini often boast charming settings with white-washed walls, blue domes, and rustic decor that perfectly captures the island's architectural aesthetics. Many of these establishments are nestled along narrow cobblestone streets, offering diners a glimpse into the island's enchanting past.

2. Local Ingredients and Cuisine: These restaurants take pride in sourcing fresh, local ingredients, showcasing the best of Santorini's agricultural and maritime resources. The cuisine is characterised by its use of olive oil, tomatoes, fava beans, capers, and unique wines, such as Assyrtiko. Seafood is also a highlight, with dishes featuring freshly caught fish and octopus.

3. Signature Dishes: Traditional Greek restaurants in Santorini offer a range of signature dishes that celebrate the island's culinary heritage. Some notable options include:

  - Santorinian Salad: A refreshing blend of tomatoes, cucumbers, capers, olives, and feta cheese, drizzled with olive oil and sprinkled with oregano.
  - Fava: A creamy dip made from split yellow peas, often served with onions, capers, and a drizzle of olive oil.
  - Seafood Delicacies: Grilled octopus, calamari, and freshly caught fish are often prepared with simple seasonings, allowing the natural flavors to shine.
  - Local Cheese: Sample artisanal cheeses like chloro (soft white cheese) or kopanisti (spicy cheese), often paired with local honey or figs.
  - Moussaka: A hearty casserole dish made with layers of eggplant, ground meat, and béchamel sauce.

4. Wine Culture: Santorini is renowned for its exceptional wines, particularly the indigenous Assyrtiko grape variety. Traditional Greek restaurants on the island take great care in curating wine lists that feature local vintages, offering diners

the opportunity to savor wines that perfectly complement their meals.

5. Cultural Experience: Dining at a traditional Greek restaurant in Santorini offers more than just a meal—it's a cultural experience. Many restaurants showcase live music, dance performances, or themed nights that celebrate Greek traditions and entertain guests.

6. Warm Hospitality: Greek hospitality, known as "philoxenia," is a hallmark of dining experiences in Santorini. Visitors can expect warm and friendly service, creating a welcoming atmosphere that adds to the overall enjoyment of the meal.

7. Scenic Views: Many traditional Greek restaurants in Santorini offer spectacular views of the caldera and the sea. This enhances the dining experience, allowing guests to soak in the island's breathtaking beauty while indulging in delectable dishes.

8. Reservations and Recommendations: Due to the popularity of traditional Greek restaurants in Santorini, it's advisable to make reservations in advance, especially during peak tourist seasons. Locals or hotel staff can often provide recommendations for authentic and lesser-known

dining spots that offer a more intimate and genuine experience.

In essence, dining at a traditional Greek restaurant in Santorini is a journey that combines exquisite flavors, cultural immersion, and stunning vistas, making it an unforgettable experience for every traveler seeking a taste of authentic Greek cuisine and hospitality.

6.2 Seafood Specialties

Santorini, renowned for its stunning landscapes and breathtaking sunsets, also offers a delectable array of seafood specialties that are a true delight for culinary enthusiasts. Nestled in the heart of the Aegean Sea, the island boasts an abundance of fresh seafood, resulting in a diverse and vibrant culinary scene. Here are some of the seafood specialties you can savour in Santorini:

1. Fried Calamari: A classic Greek dish, fried calamari is a popular appetizer on the island. Tender rings of calamari are lightly battered and fried to perfection, resulting in a crispy and flavorful dish. It's often served with a squeeze of lemon and a side of tzatziki sauce.

2. Grilled Octopus: Santorini's grilled octopus is a culinary masterpiece. The tender octopus is marinated with olive oil, lemon, and a blend of aromatic herbs, then grilled to achieve a delightful smoky flavour. It's commonly served with a drizzle of olive oil and a sprinkle of oregano.

3. Lobster Pasta: For a luxurious treat, indulge in lobster pasta, a dish that combines succulent lobster meat with al dente pasta in a flavorful tomato or garlic-infused sauce. The combination of fresh seafood and Mediterranean flavors creates a truly indulgent experience.

4. Seafood Souvlaki: Santorini offers a unique twist on the traditional souvlaki by featuring skewers of grilled seafood. These skewers may include a variety of seafood such as shrimp, fish, and squid, marinated in local herbs and spices for a burst of flavor.

5. Fresh Fish: The island's proximity to the sea ensures an abundance of fresh fish options. Local tavernas often present a catch of the day, allowing you to choose from a variety of fish such as red mullet, sea bream, and snapper. Grilled or oven-baked, the fish is often prepared simply to let its natural flavours shine.

6. Santorinian Fava: While not a seafood dish per se, Santorinian fava is a popular accompaniment to seafood. This creamy yellow split pea puree is typically served as a dip or side dish, complementing the flavours of grilled seafood perfectly.

7. Seafood Risotto: Combining the richness of seafood with the comfort of risotto, this dish offers a delightful blend of flavours and textures. A creamy risotto base is infused with the essence of the sea through the addition of shrimp, mussels, and other seafood delicacies.

8. Mussels Saganaki: A tantalising dish that showcases the Greek saganaki cooking technique, mussels saganaki features plump mussels cooked in a tomato and feta cheese sauce. This savoury dish is often paired with crusty bread for dipping.

When dining in Santorini, you can expect to savor these seafood specialties while taking in the mesmerising views of the Aegean Sea. The island's culinary scene truly captures the essence of the Mediterranean, offering a delightful fusion of flavors that are sure to leave a lasting impression on your taste buds.

6.3 Must-Try Santorinian Dishes

Santorini, a picturesque island in the Aegean Sea, offers a delightful culinary experience with its unique blend of Mediterranean flavors and local ingredients. Here are some must-try Santorinian dishes that showcase the island's gastronomic delights:

1. Fava Santorinis: This traditional dish features a creamy yellow split pea purée, often served as an appetiser. It's typically drizzled with local olive oil and topped with chopped onions, capers, and sometimes even octopus. The rich, velvety texture and distinct flavors make it a beloved starter.

2. Tomatokeftedes: These crispy tomato fritters are a culinary delight. Made with Santorini's unique cherry tomatoes, fresh herbs, and local cheese, they are deep-fried to perfection. Tomatokeftedes offer a burst of Mediterranean flavors with a slightly tangy and savoury taste.

3. Santorinian Salad: A refreshing combination of ingredients like cherry tomatoes, cucumbers, capers, onions, and olives, all drizzled with olive oil and sprinkled with crumbled feta cheese. It's a light and vibrant dish that captures the essence of the island's fresh produce.

4. Seafood Delights: Given its coastal location, Santorini offers an array of seafood dishes. Grilled octopus, calamari, and fresh fish are often cooked with simple seasonings to let the natural flavours shine through. Enjoy these dishes with stunning sea views for an unforgettable dining experience.

5. White Eggplant: Santorini is famous for its small, sweet, and slightly bitter white eggplants. These are often used to create dishes like moussaka or imam bayildi, where the eggplant is stuffed with a flavorful mixture of onions, tomatoes, and spices.

6. Santorinian Sausages (Lukaniko): These pork sausages are seasoned with a blend of spices, including orange zest, giving them a unique and delightful taste. Grilled to perfection, they are a popular street food option.

7. Pork Souvlaki: While souvlaki is a common Greek dish, Santorini's version is distinctive due to the island's local ingredients and preparation methods. Succulent pieces of marinated pork are skewered and grilled, often served with pita bread, vegetables, and a variety of sauces.

8. Vinsanto: Beyond food, Santorini offers a delightful dessert wine known as Vinsanto. Made from sun-dried Assyrtiko grapes, this sweet wine boasts rich flavors of dried fruits, nuts, and honey. It's a perfect way to conclude a meal while indulging in the island's winemaking heritage.

9. Local Cheeses: Santorini is home to unique cheeses like chloro, kopanisti, and xinomyzithra. These cheeses are used in various dishes, offering distinct textures and flavours that highlight the island's dairy craftsmanship.

10. Desserts: Indulge in traditional desserts such as baklava, a sweet pastry made with layers of filo dough and honey, or loukoumades, fried dough balls soaked in honey and sprinkled with cinnamon.

Exploring Santorini's culinary scene allows you to immerse yourself in the island's culture and history while savoring the rich flavors of its locally sourced ingredients. From appetizers to desserts, each dish tells a story that reflects the beauty and charm of this stunning Greek island.

Chapter 7. Shopping and Souvenirs

7.1 Local Handmade Crafts

Local handmade crafts in Santorini showcase the island's rich cultural heritage and artistic traditions. Renowned for its stunning landscapes, picturesque villages, and vibrant sunsets, Santorini is also a hub for artisans who create exquisite crafts that reflect the island's unique charm.

One of the most iconic crafts in Santorini is pottery. The island has a long history of ceramic production, dating back to ancient times. Visitors can find a wide range of handcrafted pottery, including decorative pieces, plates, bowls, and vases. The distinctive red and black designs often draw inspiration from the island's natural beauty, featuring motifs like waves, fish, and sunsets.

Another notable craft is jewelry-making. Local artisans craft beautiful pieces using techniques passed down through generations. Santorini's jewelry often incorporates elements from its volcanic landscape, such as lava stones, beach glass, and shells. These one-of-a-kind creations capture the essence of the island and make for memorable souvenirs.

Weaving and textiles are also integral to Santorini's artisanal scene. Skilled weavers create intricate textiles using traditional looms, producing items like rugs, tablecloths, and clothing. Many of these textiles showcase intricate patterns and designs that reflect the island's history and culture.

For those interested in culinary crafts, Santorini offers delectable food products that make for excellent souvenirs. Local delicacies such as sun-dried tomatoes, capers, and aromatic herbs are often handpicked and packaged by local artisans. These products not only represent the island's flavors but also allow visitors to take a piece of Santorini's culinary heritage home with them.

Painting and artwork are also thriving on the island, with many artists drawing inspiration from Santorini's breathtaking landscapes. From traditional scenes of whitewashed buildings perched on cliffs to contemporary interpretations of the island's beauty, the local art scene is diverse and vibrant.

Visitors can explore these crafts at various local markets, boutiques, and artisan workshops scattered throughout Santorini. Engaging with these artisans offers a unique opportunity to learn about their craft, hear stories of their heritage, and bring home a tangible piece of Santorini's artistic legacy. Whether it's pottery, jewelry, textiles, or culinary delights, Santorini's local handmade crafts provide a window into the island's soul and make for cherished mementos of a memorable visit.

7.2 Art Galleries and Boutiques

Santorini, known for its breathtaking beauty and stunning landscapes, is also a hub for art galleries and boutiques that cater to both local and international tastes. These establishments offer a diverse range of artistic expressions and handcrafted items that capture the essence of the island's charm.

Art Galleries:
Santorini's art galleries showcase an eclectic mix of contemporary and traditional art forms, often inspired by the island's unique surroundings. Visitors can explore a variety of galleries featuring works by local and international artists, including paintings, sculptures, ceramics, and photography. Many galleries also organize exhibitions and events that celebrate the fusion of modern creativity with the island's rich cultural heritage.

One notable art gallery on Santorini is the Art Space Gallery in Exo Gonia. Housed in a former winery, this gallery exhibits a collection of contemporary artworks within its rustic stone walls. It provides a serene backdrop for art enthusiasts to immerse themselves in both the art and the history of the space.

Boutiques:
Santorini's boutiques offer an array of handcrafted and artisanal products that reflect the island's distinct character. From fashion and jewelry to home decor and accessories, these boutiques present a carefully curated selection of items that highlight local craftsmanship and creativity.

Oia, a charming village known for its mesmerizing sunsets, is a haven for boutique shopping. Here, visitors can explore a myriad of boutiques that offer unique clothing, accessories, and souvenirs. The narrow cobblestone streets are lined with shops featuring everything from handwoven textiles to intricate jewelry pieces inspired by Santorini's landscape.

Artistic Influences:
The art galleries and boutiques in Santorini draw inspiration from the island's natural beauty, its

Cycladic architecture, and its captivating views of the Aegean Sea. Many artists find themselves captivated by the interplay of light and shadow, which gives rise to a vibrant spectrum of colours that often find their way onto canvases and other artistic mediums.

Local traditions and folklore also play a significant role in shaping the artistic creations found on the island. Visitors can find pieces that celebrate Santorini's history, mythology, and cultural heritage, all of which contribute to the unique character of the artworks and products on display.

In conclusion, Santorini's art galleries and boutiques offer an immersive experience for visitors seeking to explore and appreciate the island's artistic expressions. From contemporary artworks to traditional crafts, these establishments provide a glimpse into the creative soul of Santorini, allowing travelers to take home a piece of its beauty and inspiration.

Chapter 8. Nightlife and Entertainment

8.1 Bars and Beach Clubs

Santorini, a stunning Greek island in the Aegean Sea, is renowned for its breathtaking sunsets, turquoise waters, and charming villages perched atop cliffs. The island offers a variety of bars and beach clubs, each with its own unique ambiance and style. Here's an overview of some of the popular bars and beach clubs you can find in Santorini:

Bars:
1. Franco's Bar: Situated in Fira, the capital of Santorini, Franco's Bar offers panoramic views of the caldera and the azure sea. It's an excellent spot to savor cocktails while watching the famous Santorini sunset.

2. PK Cocktail Bar: Located in Oia, PK Cocktail Bar provides an enchanting atmosphere with its cosy seating and expertly crafted cocktails. The bar's vantage point offers uninterrupted views of the caldera and the charming town of Oia.

3. Two Brothers Bar: Perched atop the cliffs in Imerovigli, Two Brothers Bar is known for its relaxed ambiance and impressive cocktail menu.

Visitors can enjoy refreshing drinks and take in the stunning vistas.

4. Tropical Bar: Found in Perissa, Tropical Bar offers a vibrant beachside setting where you can enjoy tropical cocktails and live music. It's a great place to unwind and enjoy the lively atmosphere.

Beach Clubs:
1. Theros Wave Bar: Nestled on the black sand beach of Vlychada, Theros Wave Bar combines natural beauty with luxury. The club features comfortable loungers, umbrellas, and a serene setting for a relaxing beach experience.

2. Mojo Beach Bar: Situated on Kamari Beach, Mojo Beach Bar boasts a lively and vibrant ambiance. It's a popular spot for daytime lounging, with comfortable seating, music, and a variety of refreshing beverages.

3. Santo Maris Oia Beach Club: Part of the Santo Maris Oia Luxury Suites & Spa, this beach club offers an upscale experience. With its infinity pool, sunbeds, and stunning views, it's a great place to indulge in luxury by the sea.

4. Seaside by Notos: Located in Vlychada, Seaside by Notos offers a blend of sophistication and natural beauty. Visitors can enjoy a stylish beachfront setting with comfortable loungers, umbrellas, and a chic atmosphere.

5. Kamari Beach Club: Situated on Kamari Beach, this beach club offers a laid-back environment with sunbeds, umbrellas, and a variety of food and drink options. It's an ideal place to relax by the sea.

These are just a few examples of the bars and beach clubs you can find in Santorini. Whether you're looking for a relaxing beach day or a vibrant nightlife experience, Santorini offers a range of options to suit every traveller's preferences. Don't forget to take in the mesmerising views and unique atmosphere that make Santorini a world-famous destination.

8.2 Live Music and Events

Santorini, a picturesque island in the Aegean Sea, is renowned for its stunning sunsets, breathtaking landscapes, and vibrant cultural scene. Live music and events play a significant role in enhancing the island's allure, offering visitors an unforgettable experience.

1. Music Venues: Santorini boasts a variety of music venues that cater to different tastes. From beachfront bars to rooftop terraces overlooking the caldera, there's a diverse range of settings for live performances. Iconic venues like Tango Bar and Two Brothers Bar offer live music against the backdrop of the island's iconic sunset.

2. Local Music: Traditional Greek music, often accompanied by bouzouki and other instruments, can be enjoyed at local tavernas and restaurants. These authentic performances provide visitors with an opportunity to immerse themselves in the island's cultural heritage.

3. International Acts: Santorini occasionally hosts international artists who add a touch of glamour to the local music scene. Special concerts and events featuring renowned performers provide unique entertainment experiences for both tourists and locals.

4. Festivals: The island hosts various festivals celebrating music, art, and culture. The Santorini Arts Factory, for instance, organizes the Music Port Festival, featuring a diverse lineup of artists and musicians from different genres.

5. Themed Events: Many establishments on the island organize themed music nights, ranging from jazz and blues to electronic and dance music. These events create a lively atmosphere and allow visitors to enjoy their preferred genres.

6. Weddings and Private Events: Santorini's romantic ambiance makes it a sought-after destination for weddings and private events. Live music adds an enchanting touch to these celebrations, enhancing the overall experience for couples and their guests.

7. Local Musicians: Santorini has a pool of talented local musicians who often perform at various venues. Their performances showcase a mix of traditional Greek melodies and contemporary tunes, contributing to the island's vibrant music scene.

8. Cultural Diversity: The island's music scene reflects its cultural diversity, with influences from both Greek and international musical traditions. This diversity is evident in the range of music genres and performances available.

9. Summer Season: The peak tourist season, which coincides with the summer months, is when live

music and events in Santorini are most prevalent. Many venues ramp up their entertainment offerings during this time to cater to the influx of visitors.

10. Sunset Concerts: Perhaps one of the most enchanting experiences is attending a sunset concert. Musicians often perform as the sun sets over the caldera, creating a magical atmosphere that captivates both the eyes and ears.

In summary, live music and events in Santorini add a layer of enchantment to an already captivating destination. Whether you're enjoying traditional Greek melodies in a charming taverna or dancing to international beats at a beachfront party, the island's music scene offers a dynamic and diverse range of experiences that contribute to its unique allure.

Chapter 9. Practical Tips

9.1 Money and Currency

When it comes to money and currency, Santorini, like the rest of Greece, uses the Euro (€) as its official currency. The Euro is the common currency shared by the member countries of the Eurozone, which includes Greece.

In Santorini, as with other parts of Greece, you will find a variety of options for currency exchange. Banks, exchange offices, and ATMs are widely available in popular tourist areas, allowing visitors to convert their foreign currency into Euros. It's advisable to compare exchange rates and fees before making currency exchanges to ensure you're getting the best deal.

Credit and debit cards are widely accepted in Santorini, particularly in larger establishments such as hotels, restaurants, and shops. However, it's a good idea to carry some cash, especially when exploring smaller villages or markets, as not all places may accept cards.

Tipping is a common practice in Santorini, as in many parts of Greece. While not obligatory, leaving a tip of around 5-10% is appreciated for good service. Some restaurants may include a service charge in the bill, so it's a good idea to check before adding an additional tip.

When planning your trip to Santorini, it's essential to keep in mind that the cost of living and tourism-related expenses on the island can vary. Accommodation, dining, and activities can be relatively more expensive in comparison to other parts of Greece. As such, budgeting and researching beforehand will help you make the most of your visit while managing your expenses.

In summary, Santorini operates on the Euro as its official currency, and visitors have access to various currency exchange options. Credit cards are widely accepted, but it's advisable to carry some cash for smaller establishments. Tipping is customary, and budgeting for the island's relatively higher cost of living is recommended to ensure a memorable and financially sound trip.

9.2 Language and Communication

Santorini, a stunning Greek island located in the Aegean Sea, is known for its picturesque landscapes, iconic blue-domed churches, and breathtaking sunsets. While the primary language spoken in Santorini is Greek, English is widely used, particularly in tourist areas. Language and communication play vital roles in shaping the island's culture, tourism, and daily life.

Language Diversity: Greek is the official language of Santorini and is used for government, education, and official documents. The local dialect, like in many parts of Greece, may differ from standard Greek. However, due to the island's reliance on tourism, many locals are proficient in English and other languages to cater to international visitors.

Tourism and Communication: As one of the most popular tourist destinations in the world, Santorini welcomes millions of visitors each year. Consequently, effective communication in multiple languages is crucial for the island's hospitality industry. Restaurants, hotels, and tourist attractions often provide information in English, as well as other major languages, to ensure seamless interactions with visitors from various countries.

Cultural Exchange: The linguistic diversity of Santorini reflects the island's history of cultural exchange and trade. Its ancient history and geographic location have led to interactions with various civilizations, influencing its language and communication practices. While Greek remains the foundation of communication, traces of historical influences are evident in the local dialect, vocabulary, and even some customs.

Preserving Tradition: Despite the island's cosmopolitan atmosphere, efforts are made to preserve and celebrate traditional language and communication. Local festivals, such as those during Easter and other religious events, often involve traditional songs, chants, and rituals that highlight the cultural importance of language in Santorini's heritage.

Digital Communication: In recent years, digital communication has become increasingly important. Social media platforms and online resources allow locals to connect with visitors, share insights about the island, and promote tourism-related businesses. This digital landscape has further expanded the ways in which language and communication intersect with Santorini's identity.

Language and communication in Santorini are dynamic and multifaceted aspects that contribute to the island's unique character. While Greek serves as the foundation, the island's history, tourism, cultural heritage, and digital advancements all shape how languages are used and exchanged on this stunning Greek paradise.

Chapter 10. Itineraries

10.1 3 Days in Santorini

Spending three days in Santorini provides the perfect balance of relaxation, exploration, and indulgence. Here's an itinerary for your three-day visit:

Day 1: Arrival and Exploring Fira

- Morning: Arrive in Santorini, settle into your accommodation, and take in the first panoramic views of the caldera and the Aegean Sea. Start your day with a leisurely breakfast at a local café.

- Afternoon: Explore Fira, the capital of Santorini. Wander through the narrow streets, visit local shops, and immerse yourself in the unique architecture of the white-washed buildings with blue domes. Don't miss the opportunity to visit the Museum of Prehistoric Thera to learn about the island's history.

- Evening: Enjoy a traditional Greek dinner at a local taverna. As the sun sets, head to the Fira promenade to witness the famous Santorini sunset over the caldera.

Day 2: Oia and Beach Exploration

- Morning: Begin your day with a visit to Oia, one of the most picturesque villages on the island. Explore the charming streets, browse art galleries, and admire the iconic blue-domed churches. Take in the stunning views of the caldera and the endless blue sea.

- Afternoon: After lunch, head to one of Santorini's unique beaches. Perissa or Kamari are popular choices with their volcanic black sand. Relax on the beach, swim in the crystal-clear waters, or try water sports.

- Evening: Return to Oia to experience another incredible sunset. Consider booking a table at a cliffside restaurant for a romantic dinner with panoramic views.

Day 3: Volcano and Wine Tasting

- Morning: Embark on a boat tour to Nea Kameni, the volcanic island in the center of the caldera. Hike to the crater and enjoy panoramic views of the surrounding islands. Afterward, visit the thermal springs of Palea Kameni for a unique and refreshing bathing experience.

- Afternoon: Explore the local wineries of Santorini. The island is famous for its distinct volcanic soil that produces exceptional wines. Visit wineries in villages like Pyrgos or Megalochori for wine tasting sessions, accompanied by local cheeses and snacks.

- Evening: Spend your last evening indulging in a farewell dinner at a seaside restaurant. Relish in delicious Greek cuisine while reminiscing about your memorable Santorini experiences.

This itinerary is just a suggestion, and you can tailor it to your preferences. Whether you're captivated by the stunning landscapes, fascinated by the island's history, or simply seeking relaxation, Santorini offers a truly unforgettable experience over the course of three magical days.